Fierce Jobs
Deep-Sea Fishermen

by Julie Murray

Dash! LEVELED READERS
An Imprint of Abdo Zoom • abdobooks.com

2

Dash!
LEVELED READERS

Level 1 – Beginning
Short and simple sentences with familiar words or patterns for children who are beginning to understand how letters and sounds go together.

Level 2 – Emerging
Longer words and sentences with more complex language patterns for readers who are practicing common words and letter sounds.

Level 3 – Transitional
More developed language and vocabulary for readers who are becoming more independent.

THIS BOOK CONTAINS RECYCLED MATERIALS

abdobooks.com

Published by Abdo Zoom, a division of ABDO, PO Box 398166, Minneapolis, Minnesota 55439. Copyright © 2021 by Abdo Consulting Group, Inc. International copyrights reserved in all countries. No part of this book may be reproduced in any form without written permission from the publisher. Dash!™ is a trademark and logo of Abdo Zoom.

Printed in the United States of America, North Mankato, Minnesota.
052020
092020

Photo Credits: Alamy, Getty Images, iStock, Minden Pictures, Shutterstock
Production Contributors: Kenny Abdo, Jennie Forsberg, Grace Hansen, John Hansen
Design Contributors: Dorothy Toth, Neil Klinepier, Laura Graphenteen

Library of Congress Control Number: 2019956189

Publisher's Cataloging in Publication Data
Names: Murray, Julie, author.
Title: Deep-sea fishermen / by Julie Murray
Description: Minneapolis, Minnesota : Abdo Zoom, 2021 | Series: Fierce jobs | Includes online resources and index.
Identifiers: ISBN 9781098221096 (lib. bdg.) | ISBN 9781644944042 (pbk.) | ISBN 9781098222079 (ebook) | ISBN 9781098222567 (Read-to-Me ebook)
Subjects: LCSH: Deep-sea fishing--Juvenile literature. | Commercial fishing industry--Juvenile literature. | Saltwater fishing--Juvenile literature. | Hazardous occupations--Juvenile literature. | Occupations--Juvenile literature.
Classification: DDC 639.220--dc23

Table of Contents

Deep-Sea Fishermen 4

Dangerous Job 16

More Facts 22

Glossary 23

Index 24

Online Resources 24

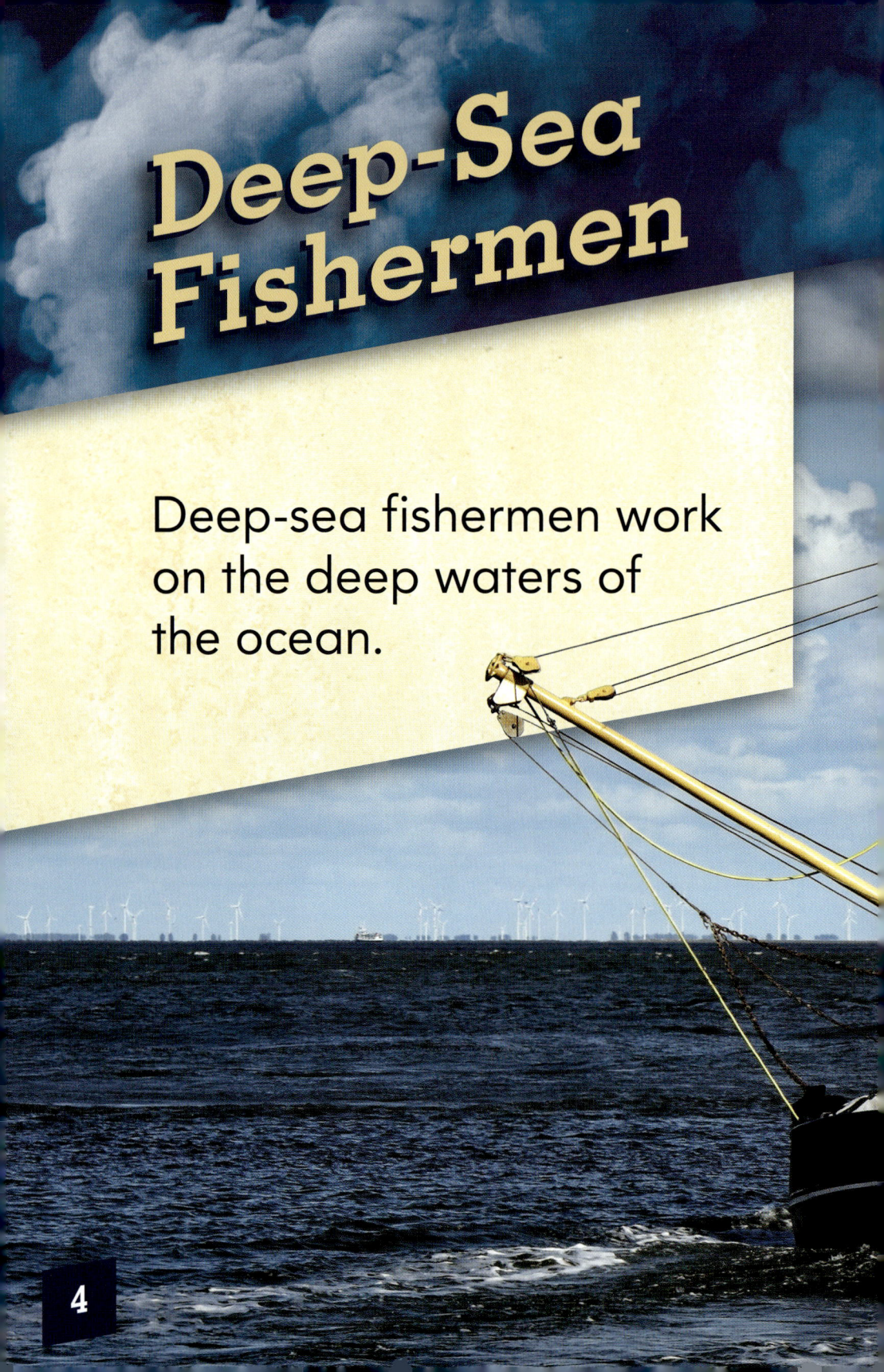

Deep-Sea Fishermen

Deep-sea fishermen work on the deep waters of the ocean.

5

They work on fishing boats. They catch many things, like crab, shrimp, and salmon.

7

Fishermen lift equipment into and out of the boat.

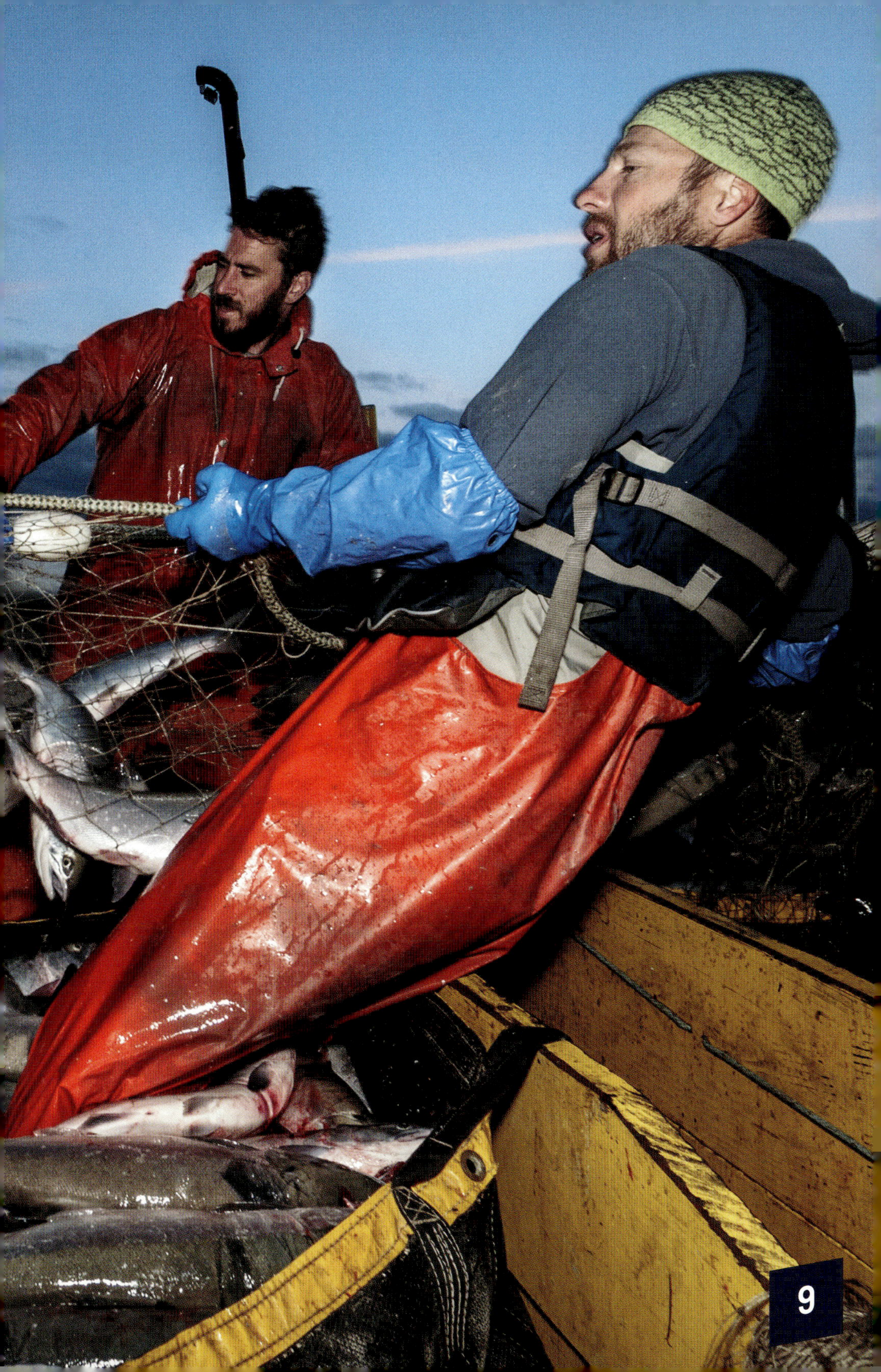

10

Fishermen use traps and **pots**. They catch crabs and lobsters with these.

11

12

They **reel out** nets. The nets target schools of fish.

14

They use **bottom trawls**. These drag along the ocean floor. Cod is caught this way.

Dangerous Job

16

Being a deep-sea fisherman is a dangerous job. Many workers are injured. Some even die on the job.

Rough seas and cold ocean water are dangerous. The most frequent cause of death is falling overboard.

19

20

The equipment onboard can be dangerous too. It is heavy. There are lots of moving parts. Fishermen risk their lives on the job!

More Facts

- In 2007, an Alaskan fisherman was 26 times more likely to die on the job compared to the national average.

- Many swordfish are caught with a longline. A longline can have more than 10,000 hooks on it!

- *The Deadliest Catch* television show highlights the dangers of the job.

Glossary

bottom trawl – a large, tapered net with a wide mouth and a small end that is weighted and dragged across the ocean floor in order to catch fish. Some consider this a destructive form of fishing.

pot – a trap that is put into the water to bait and catch fish, lobsters, and crabs.

reel out – to unwind from a reel.

Index

bottom trawl 15

casualties 17, 18

catches 6, 11, 15

dangers 17, 18, 21

equipment 8, 11, 15, 21

injuries 17

nets 13, 15

ocean 4, 18

Online Resources

Booklinks
NONFICTION NETWORK
FREE! ONLINE NONFICTION RESOURCES

To learn more about deep-sea fishermen, please visit **abdobooklinks.com** or scan this QR code. These links are routinely monitored and updated to provide the most current information available.